Practical
Karate

Defense Against an
Unarmed Assailant

Practical
Karate 2

*Defense Against an
Unarmed Assailant*

M. Nakayama
Donn F. Draeger

Tuttle Publishing
Boston • Rutland, Vermont • Tokyo

Disclaimer

The adoption and application of the material offered in this book is at the reader's discretion and sole responsibility. The Author and Publisher of this book are not responsible in any manner whatsoever for any injury that may occur indirectly or directly from the use of this book. Since the physical activities described herein may be too strenuous in nature for some readers to engage in safely, please consult a physician prior to training. The specific self-defense practices illustrated in this book may not be justified in every particular situation or under applicable federal, state or local law. Neither the Author or the Publisher make any warranty or representation regarding the legality or appropriateness of any technique mentioned in this book.

Library of Congress Catalog Card Number: 98-87646
ISBN 0-8048-0482-6

DISTRIBUTED BY

NORTH AMERICA
Tuttle Publishing
RR 1 Box 231-5
North Clarendon, VT 05759
Tel: (802) 773-8930
Tel: (800) 526-2778

SOUTHEAST ASIA
Berkeley Books Pte. Ltd.
5 Little Road #08-01
Singapore 536983
Tel: (65) 280-3320
Fax: (65) 280-6290

JAPAN
Tuttle Shokai Ltd.
1-21-13, Seki
Tama-ku, Kawasaki-shi
Kanagawa-ken 214, Japan
Tel: (044) 833-0225
Fax: (044) 822-0413

First edition
07 06 05 04 03 02 01   00 99 98   10 9 8 7 6 5 4 3 2 1

Printed in Singapore

TABLE OF CONTENTS

AUTHORS' FOREWORD

THIS BOOK is written for every male and brings to him a chance to improve his personal self-defense abilities without engaging in the severe discipline and dedication to daily training required by classical *karate*. It is not intended to be an exhaustive survey of *karate* methods, but it does set down the "meat" necessities for practical application. In choosing this book's methods and techniques, careful consideration was given to the practice time available to the average person. The many complex movements of classical *karate* can never be efficiently learned by the casual practitioner who, by less than daily training, can never attain the flexibility and reflex action essential to the acrobatic movements of a *karate* expert. Therefore, a simplified, direct method of self-defense is necessary.

You will notice that the arrangement of this text is a categorized collection of self-defense situations and recommended *karate* responses. Here you can readily find common self-defense problems and an efficient response thereto. If you have already studied and practiced the necessary *karate* fundamentals found in Book one of this series, the situations in this volume will be easy to learn. Otherwise, after reading about the situation and response herein, you may find it necessary to turn to Book one to find the movements and exercises which are necessary to make these responses work effectively.

All methods described in this book are workable *karate* self-defense responses based on facing an unarmed assailant. The subjects of self-defense against an armed assailant or multiple assailants are not treated, since they are highly specialized and beyond the scope of this book. These topics will be covered in Books three and four. Likewise, self-defense for females is not included due to the limitations of their physical abilities and restrictions of dress. This subject will be covered in Book five of this series.

The reader is reminded that even mastery of what is outlined in this text *will* not make him invincible in personal encounters, but it will certainly better prepare him should defense of his life or that of others become necessary. He is further reminded that mere reading, together with one or two rehearsals of each response in this book, will not produce results.

The authors are indebted to the Japan Karate Association, Tokyo, Japan, for the use of their facilities and hereby acknowledge with pleasure the assistance of those members and officials who have made this book possible. Additional thanks is due to the excellent photographic skills of Akira Kasahara, which has given this book its illustrations, and to James S. Bregman, a student of combative arts who posed as the "assailant" in the illustrations.

Tokyo, Japan

M. NAKAYAMA

DONN F. DRAEGER

8

PREFACE

KARATE is a martial art developed by people who were prohibited the use of weapons, thus making it a *defensive* art. When one is attacked, the empty hands (which the word *karate* implies) are quite sufficient to defend oneself if one is highly skilled in the art. However, to become highly skilled takes exacting discipline, both mental and physical. The main purpose of this series of six books is to avoid the advanced techniques of *karate* which require many years of study and instead to describe simplified *karate* technique as easy-to-learn responses to typical self-defense situations.

Karate is highly esteemed as a sport, self-defense, and as a physical attribute for athletics in general. It is becoming increasingly popular in schools, offices, factories, law enforcement agencies and the armed services, varying in degree as required by the respective wants and needs.

In response to the many requests for treatment of *karate* purely as a defensive system, it is hoped that the information contained in this series of six books will be more than sufficient to meet these requests. In conclusion, if readers of this series of books will fully understand the principles and ideals of *karate*, taking care to use its techniques with discretion, they will reflect great credit to this magnificent art.

Zentaro Kosaka

ZENTARO KOSAKA
Former Foreign Minister
of Japan
Director, Japan Karate Association

9

THE FIRST and most complete and authoritative text on *karate* in the English language, titled *Karate: The Art of "Empty Hand" Fighting*, by Hidetaka Nishiyama and Richard C. Brown, instructor and member of the Japan Karate Association respectiely, made its appearance in 1960. It presents *karate* in its three main aspects—a healthful physical art, an exciting sport, and an effective form of self-defense. As such, it is considered the standard textbook of the Japan Karate Association and adequately serves both as a reference and instructional manual for novice and expert alike.

Many students of *karate* find the study of classical *karate* somewhat impractical in modern Western society, chiefly because time limitations prohibit sufficient practice. These students generally desire to limit their interpretations of *karate* to self-defense aspects. With this sole training objective in mind, a series of six Books is being prepared which describes in simplified form, the necessary *karate* movements for personal defense that can be learned by anybody of average physical abilities.

The authors, M. Nakayama, Chief Instructor of the Japan Karate Association and Donn F. Draeger, a well-known instructor of combative arts, bring a balanced, practical, and functional approach to *karate,* based on the needs of Western society. As a specialized series of *karate* texts, these are authentic books giving full and minute explanations of the practical art of self-defense. All movements are performed in normal daily dress and bring the performer closer to reality.

Today, *karate* is attracting the attention of the whole world and is being popularized at an amazing rate. I sincerely hope that this series of books will be widely read as a useful reference for the lovers of *karate* all over the world. It is further hoped that the techniques shown in this series of books need never be used by any reader, but should an emergency arise making their use unavoidable, discretion in application should be the keynote.

MASATOMO TAKAGI
Standing Director and
Head of the General Affairs
Department of the Japan
Karate Association

Practical
Karate

*Defense Against an
Unarmed Assailant*

ESSENTIAL POINTS

1. Never underestimate your assailant. Always assume he is dangerous.

2. Stepping, weight shifting, and body turning are the keys to avoiding an assailant's attack and bringing him into position for your counterattack.

3. Turn your body as a unit, not in isolated parts, for maximum effect.

4. If the ground is rough, bumpy, or slick, you may be unable to maneuver as you would like. Simple weight shifting and twisting of your hips may be all that is possible. Don't get too fancy in your footwork.

5. Your body can only act efficiently in *karate* techniques if you make it a stable foundation, working from braced feet and a balanced position as you deliver your blow.

6. Coordinate your blocking or striking action to the assailant's target area with your stepping, weight shifting, and body turning for maximum effect.

7. Do not oppose superior power with power, but seek to harmonize it with your body action and direct it to your advantage.

8. Seek to deliver your striking actions to the assailant's anatomical weak points (vital points) rather than to hard, resistant areas.

9. After delivering the striking action to your assailant's target area, you must never loose sight of him and you should be constantly alert for a continuation of his attack.

10. Use discretion in dealing out punishment to any assailant. Fit the degree of punishment to the situation.

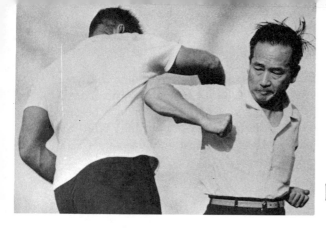

Chapter One
FRONTAL ATTACKS

AN ASSAILANT'S unarmed attack from the front can take various forms. Commonly such attacks include seizing, holding the arms or portions of garments, hugging, choking, punching, striking, kicking, or tackling. Frequently, combinations of these tactics are used with effective results against an untrained individual.

The person highly trained in *karate* techniques need not fear any such attack and is able to meet such emergencies with confidence. Yet, there is a considerable difference between the highly trained and the average citizen. The situations and the appropriate responses shown in this chapter are specially selected for the average citizen and cover the necessary principles to successfully meet common eventualities of frontal unarmed attack.

It is essential that the responses described in this chapter be practiced with a partner. In the beginning, the practice should be very carefully regulated by performing the necessary movements in slow motion until the exact performance is completely understood. By gradually increasing the speed of the response as your training partner "attacks," you will build an automatic response. Frequent practice—a few minutes a day several days a week—will aid this development.

As suggested in this text, practice should be performed in normal daily dress. Do not make the mistake of practicing only on a smooth, flat surface such as a gym floor, but try to make these responses on grass, gravel, and paved and unpaved surfaces so that you will be prepared for the situation as it could happen.

While the responses described are given in terms of one side—performing either on the right or left sides—in many instances the other side may be learned by simply reversing the instructions.

Finally, in the execution of the responses, *never* assume that your first response will satisfy the situation. Rather assume a constant alertness which will enable you to continue your attack should it become necessary. The price of a lack of alertness may be your life! While the responses of this book may be directed toward only one target area, other opportunities should be studied.

Situation: An assailant has grasped your right sleeve or wrist with his left hand from the front and is threatening to use force against you. You have plenty of room to move about.

Response: At his grasp, center your weight
with legs somewhat wider apart than usual.
Be sure to advance the leg on the side which
the assailant is grasping (right shown). Watch
the assailant carefully. Prepare a tight fist
with the left hand, knuckles down, holding
it close to the left hip. (See picture, page 15.)

Keep rearmost foot (left shown) firmly
planted on the ground as you shift weight to
that leg. Slide the right foot back a short distance as shown in the diagram, being careful
not to bring the feet together. At the same
time, using the drawing power of your
weight, shift to the left leg, pull the arm
across the front of your body in a downward
direction (in line with an extension of the
assailant's left arm), rotating the wrist toward your thumb as you do this. Keep your
chin tight to the chest as you pull. (See
picture, left above.)

As the right arm comes free from the assailant's grasp, make a tight fist. Continue withdrawing the right arm and, with a circular motion, bring it up across the chest, knuckles up. (See pictures.)

If necessary, strike the assailant in the face area (chin, mouth, nose, temple, eyes) with the right hand used either as a Back Fist, Bottom Fist, or Knife-hand. (See picture, page 18.) Do this by stepping forward with the right foot between the feet of the assailant (see diagram), using that shift of the body weight forward to give the striking action terrific power.

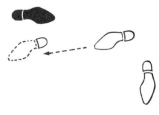

Key Points: Both your arm release and the striking action must be timed with the shift of the body weight caused by your stepping movements, or the response may be ineffective. Notice also that the arm release and striking is done circularly, pivoting on the shoulder, not the elbow. After striking, keep alert and have the left fist ready for parrying and/or additional striking action.

18

Situation: An assailant has grasped your left sleeve or wrist with his right hand from the front in an attempt to pull you. Your movement backward is limited or impossible.

19

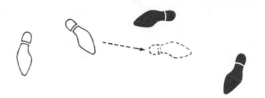

Response: At his grasp (see top left) step in between his legs with the left foot as shown in the diagram. As you step in, use the captured wrist as a pivot point, and shove the left elbow, point first, forward toward your assailant. (See picture, right.)

Continue driving the elbow forward, putting your body weight behind it. (See picture, page 21.)

The elbow must be shoved forward with a quick, snapping action, with the wrist remaining almost in place or possibly pulled backward toward your body a bit. (See diagram.)

As your assailant's grasp is torn loose, the elbow point is raised high and the other hand begins to form a fist.

Strike the assailant in the solar plexus area by driving your elbow hard forward in a straight line toward the target. As you strike, shift your body weight forward to aid in the force of the striking. Simultaneous with the striking, draw the other arm close alongside the body, hand held in a tight fist, knuckles upward, at the hip. (See picture on page 22.)

Key Points: Lower the hips slightly as you strike the target. The arm release and the striking action must be timed with the shift of the body weight and lowering action or the response may be ineffective. After striking, keep alert and have the right fist ready for parrying and/or additional striking action.

Situation: An assailant has grasped your right sleeve or wrist with his right hand from the front and is threatening you. You have plenty of room to move.

Response: At his grasp, center your weight to keep your balance. Watch your assailant carefully. (See picture, page 23.) Step your left foot behind the assailant's right foot, toes pointing inward, as shown in the diagram.

As you step forward with your left foot, bend your knees slightly. Pivot your right foot slightly to the right rear as shown in the diagram, and at the same time withdraw the right arm downward (in line with an extension of the assailant's right arm) with a snapping motion of the forearm. The palm is rotated upward against the assailant's thumb during this action and the elbow must be kept close to the right hip. Keep the chin tight against your chest as you withdraw the arm. Begin to raise your free left arm, bringing it across the body, knuckles outward. The weight is now shifted over your right leg. (See three pictures, page 25.)

24

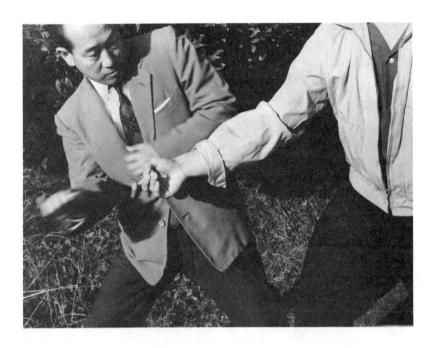

As the assailant's grasp is torn loose, bring the left arm fully across your chest, knuckles outward, palm near the right shoulder. The arm must be raised above the assailant's right arm.

If necessary, strike the assailant in the chest (throat, chin, mouth, nose, temple, eyes) with the left elbow or the left hand used as a Back fist or Bottom fist. Time the striking action with a shift of the body from the right foot to the left foot to give the striking action terrific power. This action is shown on page 26.

Key Points: Both the arm release and the striking action must be timed with the shift of the body weight, or the response may be ineffective. Notice also that the arm release requires a rotation of the right palm, upward against the assailant's right thumb. If the assailant's grasp is not broken completely, it does not effect the striking action seriously. After striking, keep alert.

26

Situation: As assailant has grasped your right wrist with both of his hands from the front in an attempt to pull you. You have plenty of room to move.

Response 1: At his grasp, keep your balance and carefully watch the assailant. (See picture, page 27.) Quickly reach forward between the assailant's arms, passing your left hand over the assailant's right arm, clasping the hands tightly together as shown in the upper left picture. Immediately step directly forward with the right foot, knee slightly bent, to a position between the assailant's feet shown in the diagram. Shift your weight to that foot as you pull back with both hands (follow picture sequence at top of these two pages), and drive the right elbow forward. The elbow comes up high as the assailant's grasp is broken.

Strike the assailant on the chin with the right elbow by coming up forcibly with the right elbow and driving the body slightly upward. This action can be seen on page 30.

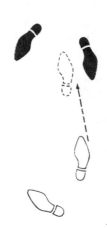

Key Points: The escape action is a prying one, with leverage against the assailant's grasp and should be coordinated with your step forward. Do not tug to release yourself.

28

Response 2: At his grasp, keep your balance and carefully watch the assailant. (See picture, page 27.) Quickly reach forward with the left hand, under the assailant's right arm, and clasp your hands tightly together. (See pictures below.) Immediately step directly forward with your right foot, knee slightly bent, to a position between the assailant's feet as in the diagram on page 28. Shift your weight to that foot as you pull the hands backward and drive the right elbow forward to loosen his grasp, as in the picture sequence below.

Strike the assailant in the solar plexus by shifting your weight forward and driving your elbow hard into the target area. This action can be seen on page 30.

Key Points: The escape action is a prying one with leverage against the assailant's grasp and should be coordinated with your forward step. Do not tug to release yourself.

30

Situation: An assailant has grasped both of your wrists from the front. You have plenty of room to move as he menaces you.

31

Response: At his grasp, brace yourself and keep your balance. (See page 31.) Quickly step backward with your right foot, toes pointing slightly outward as in the diagram.

Begin to cross your arms, passing your right arm under your left, raising the left elbow slightly to permit passage of the right arm. (Top picture.)

Fold the left arm across your body, palm down, fingers pointing to your right as your right arm comes into position under the assailant's right wrist. (Follow picture se-

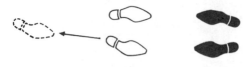

quence.) Flex your right wrist so that the fingers point upward and the knife edge of that hand is pressed hard against the right wrist of the assailant.

Continue pressing hard against the right wrist of the assailant with the knife edge of your right hand as you pull the left arm loose from the assailant's right hand grasp and quickly grasp the assailant's right wrist with your right hand. Place your left hand on the assailant's right arm at a point just above his left elbow.

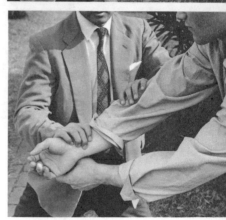

Your assailant's balance is broken to his left front corner and you are braced solidly against him. This position is better shown in the picture below.

If necessary, kick your assailant in the groin, knee, or shin with the ball or tip of your shoe or your knee by pulling him further off balance, with both hands, in the direction of your right rear corner as you kick forward to the target area. This action is shown on page 34. After kicking him, keep alert.

Key Points: You must press your right hand knife edge hard against the assailant's right wrist as you coordinate this force with the pull of the left arm to break his grasp. Unbalance the assailant by pulling strongly in the direction of your right rear corner as you begin the kick. With a tall assailant, do not try to kick above his knee.

Situation: An assailant has seized your wrist in judo fashion and is attempting to bring you under submission by twisting your wrist. You have plenty of room to move about.

35

Response: As the assailant applies pressure to your wrist (see page 35), keep your wrist in place by moderate resistance.

Pivot your right foot on the ball of the foot and at the same time, swing the left foot behind you in an arc, stepping it to a new position as shown in the diagram.

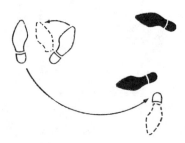

As you swing your body around (see left picture, page 37), lift your left arm in front of your body, parallel to the ground, knuckles upward, and begin to make a tight fist with that hand. Lower the hips slightly.

Coming into place in your new position, keep the captured wrist near the back of your head as you raise the left arm across your face, knuckles upward, in a tight fist. (See right picture, page 37.)

Strike the assailant in the ribs with a Elbow Sideward Strike by chopping your arm direct to the target. Twist your hips in the direction of the striking action. The striking action can be seen on page 38.

Key Points: Your response to this effective attack must be applied early if there is to be any chance of success. The stepping, twisting, and striking action must be unified in one smooth effort and done quickly. Any hesitation during the route will cause the response to fail.

Alternate striking actions can include an Elbow Sideward Strike to the side of the assailant's head or the use of a Back or Bottom Fist to the head or face area, as shown on page 38.

Situation: An assailant has tackled you from the front in an attempt to pick you up and knock you to the ground. The assailant's head and face are sufficiently protected from your kneeing counterattack. You have plenty of room to move about.

39

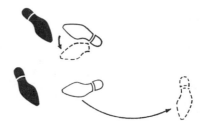

Response: As he tackles you, keep your balance (see page 39), and take advantage of his forward momentum which is driving you backward by quickly pivoting the right foot slightly to your left and then firmly weighting that leg. Immediately twist the hips to your left by withdrawing the left leg in a wide, circular step to your rear. As the left leg comes into place, center your body weight to give you balance as shown in the diagram. Raise your right arm so as to clear your elbow above your charging assailant's back. (See pictures.)

Strike your assailant at any point along the line of his spinal column extending downward from the base of his skull to his upper back, using an Elbow Downward Strike. As you strike, lower your hips by bending your knees slightly and withdrawing your left arm tightly to your left side, knuckles down. (See picture at top of next page.)

Key Points: Withdraw your leg on the same side of your body that the assailant places his head while attacking you. Time this withdrawal and twist of the hips with the momentum of his tackle. Notice that the withdrawn foot makes a large arc backward and brings you to a wide stance for stability. Time the striking with the lowering of your hips and notice also that the striking arm requires a tight fist, palm facing you.

If you catch the assailant in the early stages of his tackling, you may be able to stop him with a blow using the Bottom Fist at the base of his skull. If he tackles you head-on, you can knee him in the face. (See pictures, page 42.)

42

Situation: An assailant of about your same stature has grasped your right lapel with his left hand from the front, and is beginning to strike you with a "roundhouse" right.

43

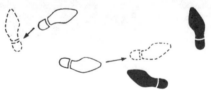

Response: At his grasp, do not tug to free yourself, but keep your balance. (See page 43.) Step forward with your right foot, toes pointing toward the assailant's right foot, to a position between his legs as you step circularly to your rear with your left foot as shown in the diagram.

This action will turn your body so you are looking at the assailant's right fist. As you step forward, pass your right arm over the assailant's left arm which is grasping your lapel. Your right hand is held in a tight

fist. Draw the left arm close to your left hip, also in a tight fist, knuckles down. (See picture, page 44.)

As the assailant strikes with his right hand, parry the blow with your right Forearm Block. (See picture.)

Strike the assailant in the solar plexus or face area with your right elbow by bringing your right hand parry down sharply, elbow first, into the target. Twist your hand, knuckles up, during this striking action and lower your hips by bending your knees slightly to give your blow more force. This action can be seen on page 46.

45

Key Points: This response is best used against an assailant who is about your same stature or one who is gripping your lapel low enough to permit you to pass your right arm over his grip.

46

Situation: An assailant has grasped your right lapel with his left hand from the front and is preparing to strike you with a straight punch. You have plenty of room to move about.

Response: At his grasp, do not tug to free yourself, but keep your balance, as in the picture on page 47. Step backward with your left leg, a bit circularly. Center your weight and brace your feet as in the diagram.

As you step backward, twist your body to the left and push your right shoulder hard against the assailant's left hand grasp. Your left arm is close to the body with an open hand, palm upward, fingers together during this action. (See picture.)

As the assailant throws his straight punch with his right hand, drive your hand, fashioned as a Hand Spear, just inside of his punching arm (see pictures, page 49) deflecting it.

Then ram your hand straight into his throat or eyes. Your legs must be firmly braced and kept in place during this thrusting. This action can be seen on page 50.

48

Key Points: In the same situation, if you are unable to move backward, apply a shearing action using the palm-heel of your right hand hard against the assailant's left arm at a point just slightly above the elbow and the palm heel of your left arm hard against the assailant's left wrist. (See lower pictures, page 50.) Time these blows, striking hard together, as you twist your body slightly to your left.

This technique is easy to use if the assailant is taller than you or is grasping high on your lapel or collar.

49

Situation: An assailant has grasped both your lapels from the front and has backed you up against a wall, threatening you.

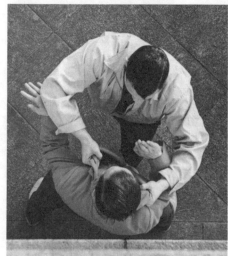

Response: At his grasp, do not tug to free yourself, but keep your balance. (See picture, page 51.) Keep your feet in place, but pivot both of them slightly to your left as you release your grasp of his arms. (See the diagram.) Drive your right arm up under his left arm from the inside as shown in the top picture.

Pivot your feet to the right as shown in the diagram, twisting your hips to the right as you pivot. Sweep the outer edge of your right forearm hard against the inside of the assailant's left arm. Simultaneous with this action, push hard against the assailant's right elbow with the flat of your left hand from the bottom as in the lower picture.

52

Break your assailant off balance by combined action of your hip twist, and your two arms as in the above picture.

If necessary, strike your assailant in the groin or abdominal region with a roundhouse knee kick by swinging your bent left knee in a short arc direct to his target area. If your assailant twists, your target may be his ribs. (See picture, page 54.)

Key Points: Your pivotal foot action, hip twist, and arm action must be timed as a unified effort or it may lessen the effectiveness of this response. Lower your hips slightly as you use arm action. An alternate action uses either the Right Back Fist or Palm-heel to the assailant's face area from the positions in the figures on page 52.

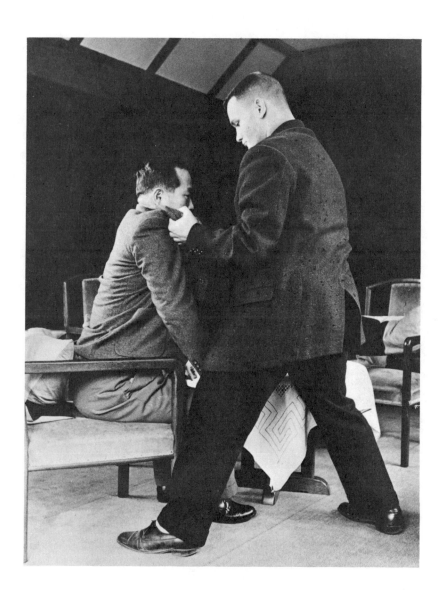

Situation: You are seated and an assailant has grasped both your lapels from the front in an attempt to drag you out of your chair, stand you up, and strike you.

Response 1: At the assailant's grasp, keep your balance and do not try to tug or break away from his hold on your lapels. Keep both your hands in your lap, ready for action. (See picture, page 55.)

Deliver a kick with the toe or ball of your shoe directly to the assailant's shin, knee, or inside of his calf, or drive your foot edge hard downward along his shinbone and stamp into his instep. (See pictures.)

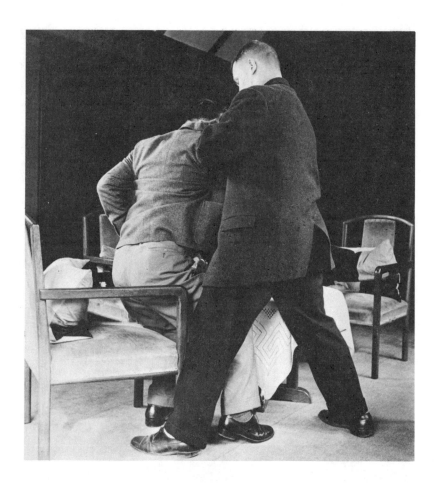

Response 2: At the assailant's grasp, keep your balance and do not try to tug away or break his hold on your lapels. Keep both hands in your lap ready for action, as in the picture on page 55.

As your assailant pulls you to your feet, rise, keeping your balance. Turn slightly toward the side of the assailant's rear foot (right shown). (See picture above.)

Drive a Right Elbow Forward Strike into the assailant's mid-section as you twist your body to the left. Withdraw your left arm along your body and form a fist, knuckles down at your left hip. Keep this ready for another attack if necessary. This action can be seen on page 58.

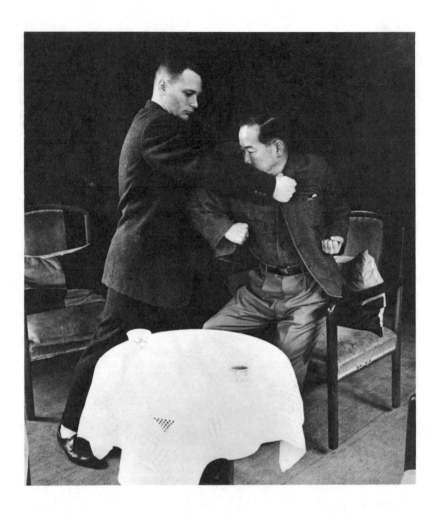

Key Points: Allow your assailant to keep his grasp of your lapels and thus keep his hands occupied.

In Response 1, be extremely careful after you deliver the kick and be prepared for a punch from the assailant if he releases his grasp.

In Response 2, as you rise, be careful to avoid a kneeing attack from the assailant.

You may deliver Response 3 (not shown) by driving your Forefist or Bottom Fist to his groin as you remain seated.

58

Situation: An assailant has grasped your belt from the front with his left hand and is preparing to land a "haymaker" right. You have plenty of room to move about.

59

Response: Keep your balance as the assailant holds or pulls you forward with his left hand. (See picture, page 59.)

As he swings his right hand to strike you, begin to step backward with your left foot and start driving a Rising Block with your left forearm hard against the inside of the assailant's right forearm. (See picture above.)

As your left foot comes into its new position—toes pointing slightly outward as in the diagram—brace yourself firmly.

Your new position and rising block will deflect the assailant's "haymaker" right and bring him slightly forward, off balance. Form an open hand with your right hand, palm upward, at your right hip. (See picture above.)

Strike your assailant in the face area (chin, mouth, nose) by delivering a hard rising Palm-heel blow. During this action, keep your feet in place as in the diagram. This action can be seen on page 62.

Key Points: Do not try to break loose from your assailant's grasp, but as you step backward with your left foot, pivot slightly to the left, using the assailant's point of grasp on your belt as the pivot point.

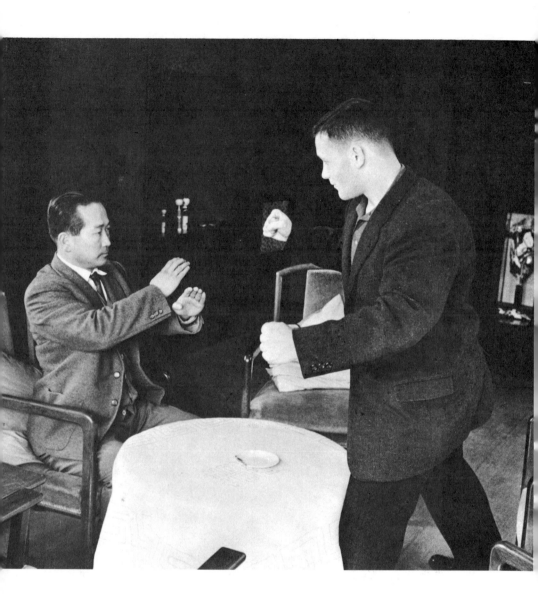

Situation: An assailant, standing in front of you, is threatening you with a straight right-hand punch to the face as you sit in a chair.

Response: Keep your eye on the assailant and do not try to get to your feet. Raise your hands, *open handed*, in front of your body, feet braced firmly on the floor. (See picture, page 63.)

As the assailant throws his punch at your face, drive a hard X-block upward against his punching arm, keeping your left hand crossed in front of your right hand, deflecting his punch upward away from your face, as in the picture above. Keep contact against his punching right

arm with your left hand as you free your right hand, *open handed*, and raise it high to your right side near your right ear, palm outward. (See picture, above.)

Grasp his punching arm with your left hand and pull it sharply downward toward your left rear, bringing him off balance. Strike him in the face, ear, or temple area with a Knife-hand formed by your right hand. This action can be seen on page 66.

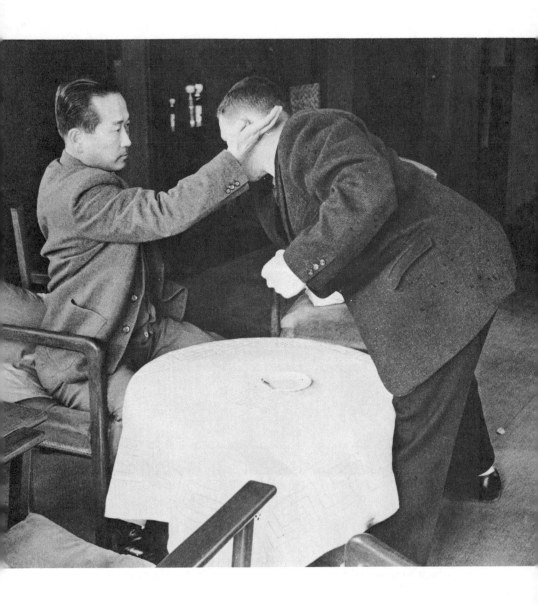

Key Points: The grasp of the assailant's punching arm followed by the downward and rear pull is necessary to unbalance the assailant and bring him into range for your Knife-hand blow.

66

Situation: An assailant has grasped your neck with both hands from the front in an attempt to strangle you. You have plenty of room to move about.

67

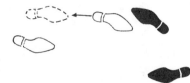

Response: As the assailant attempts to choke you, keep your balance, as in the picture on page 67. Step backward with your right foot as shown in the diagram.

Drive your hands (which are pressed tightly together palm to palm, fingers pointing upward) upward with your arms forming a Wedge Block. Continue this upward drive of your arms and as you feel the assailant's grasp loosening, separate your hands a bit and grasp the assailant's arms. Weight your rear leg (right) and begin shifting your weight to bring the assailant forward and off balance by sliding your advanced foot (left) backward alongside your rear foot (right). (See picture above and lower right, page 69.)

If your assailant rushes forward, pushing you back as you slide your left foot back, step well back on that foot and shift your weight onto it. (See three top figures.)

Shift your weight to the left leg and lift your right leg, bending it at the knee so that your right thigh is parallel to the ground. Grasp your assailant's arms tightly at a point near his elbows, as shown below.

Kick the assailant in the shin, knee, groin, or abdominal region by delivering a forward snap-kick with your right leg, using the ball of your foot as the striking point. Quickly return your kicking leg to its former rearmost position. This action can be seen on page 70.

Key Points: In using the wedge action, do not separate your elbows beyond the sides of your body for it will weaken the action. Shifting your body weight from your originally weighted rear right leg to the left leg as it comes sliding into place must be a strong action in order to break the assailant's balance and to open him for your kicking attack. Bend your knees. If this is difficult to achieve, leave him in place and use your knee to strike him in the groin or abdominal region.

70

Situation: An assailant has taken you into a side headlock on your left side, twisting hard against your neck in an attempt to sling you to the ground or bring you to submission. You have little room to move.

Response: As the assailant applies pressure to your neck and begins to sling you to his front, raise your free right arm, making an open hand, fingers together. (See page 71.)

As your body loosens in the headlock, form your hand as shown in the diagram below and raise it forward of, but in direct line with, his groin region. (See pictures, page 73.)

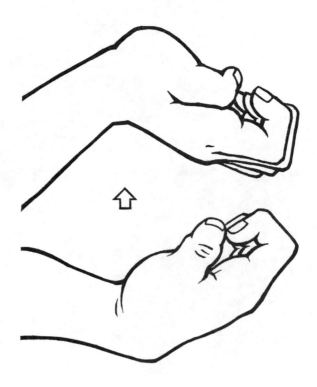

Strike your assailant by driving your Palm-
heel into his groin region by the action shown
in the diagram opposite. This is a thrusting,
or snapping action to give added force to your
Palm-heel. The striking action can be seen
on page 74.

Key Points: The Palm-heel snapping action must be coordinated with the driving thrust of your hand into the target. An alternate attack can be delivered by thrusting your Hand Spear into the assailant's eyes.

74

Situation: An assailant has grasped your right lapel with his left hand from the front and is attempting to knee you in the groin with his right leg.

75

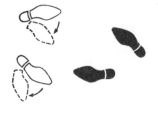

Response: At his grasp, stand fast and maintain your balance should he attempt to pull you forward. (See picture, page 75.) As the assailant begins to drive his knee forward, quickly pivot your feet slightly to your right, firmly weighting your legs. Immediately lower your hips and thrust your body slightly to your right rear corner as shown in the diagram. Twist your hips to the right and begin driving your left arm downward as a Downward Block on a line just inside of the assailant's attacking leg as you draw your right arm back alongside your right side, making a tight fist, knuckles down. (See picture above.)

Brace your feet firmly on the ground and parry the assailant's attacking right knee outward with your left arm, at a point just below your elbow. You are now fully twisted to the right. Your right fist is poised to strike. (See picture above.)

Strike your assailant in the solar plexus or rib area with your right Forefist by quickly twisting your hips to the left. Your feet stay in place, but pivot as shown in the diagram. Your left arm leaves its parry position and is drawn slightly to your left rear to assist your twist. This action can be seen on page 78.

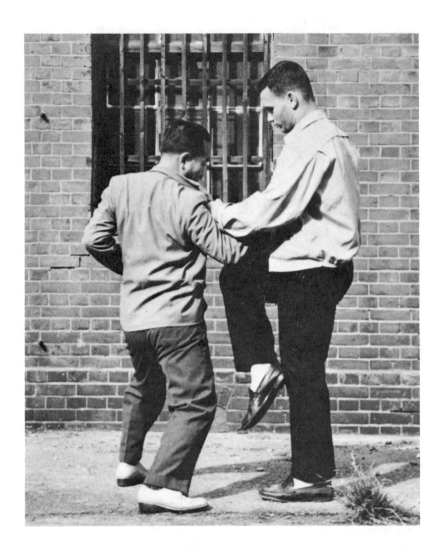

Key Points: It is important that you do not pivot too quickly; that is, before the assailant begins his kicking or kneeing attack, for this will warn the assailant and allow him to change his attack. Time this pivotal action carefully with the assailant's kick. If the assailant's grasp is low on your lapel or jacket, your striking action with your right Forefist can pass over his grasping arm.

Chapter Two
REAR ATTACKS

BEING ATTACKED by an unarmed assailant from the rear presents a more serious threat than a frontal unarmed attack, for generally it is a complete surprise and works to the disadvantage of the intended victim. These attacks, like their frontal counterparts, consist of seizing and holding the arms or garments, hugging, choking, punching, or striking, kicking, or tackling. Combinations of these methods make the rear attack extremely effective against an untrained person, and special attention must be given to the defenses and counter measures.

The person highly trained in *karate* technique meets such emergencies with confidence. The average citizen does not possess such skills. The situations and responses shown in this chapter are not exhaustive, but are specially selected for the average citizen and cover the necessary movements to meet the common eventualities of sneak, unarmed attacks from the rear.

It is essential that the responses described in this chapter be practiced with a partner. In the beginning the practice should be very carefully regulated by performing the necessary movements in slow motion until the exact performance is completely understood. By gradually increasing the speed of the response as your training partner "attacks," you will build an automatic response. A few minutes spent in practice several times a week will aid in this development.

Practice in normal daily dress. Do not make the mistake of practicing only on a smooth, flat surface such as a gym floor, but get out on the grass and paved and unpaved surfaces so you will more closely approach the real situation as it might happen.

Situations and responses are given in terms of one side—either right or left—but in many instances the other side may be learned by simply reversing the instructions.

Finally, in the execution of the responses, *never* assume that your first response will satisfy the situation. Rather assume a constant alertness which will enable you to continue your attack should it become necessary. The price of lack of alertness may be your life!

Situation: An assailant has grasped your collar or the back of your coat from the rear with his right hand and is pulling you backward. You have plenty of room to move about.

Response 1: At his grasp, as shown in the photo below, keep your balance. Step backward with your left foot, slightly on a diagonal with your toes pointing toward the assailant's left foot. Shift your weight to your right foot (see diagram at right) and fold your left arm across your body, hand formed as a Knife-hand, thumb up near your right ear, palm turned inward. Watch your assailant. (See upper pictures, page 83.)

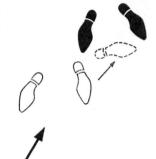

Strike your assailant with a left-handed Knife-hand directly to the neck, throat, or face area by shifting your weight more to your right foot and whipping your left arm, from the elbow, directly into the target. Keep your right fist at your right hip, knuckles down, ready to strike if necessary. (See upper picture, page 84.)

Response 2: At the assailant's grasp, keep your balance. Shift your weight to your right leg and begin lifting your left leg, knee upward. (See picture, middle of page 83.) Drive your left leg in a stamping action to the as-

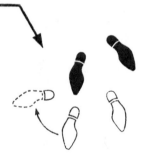

sailant's knee, shin, or instep using your Foot Edge hard against the target. The striking action can be seen on page 84, similar to Response 3, but using the right leg.

Response 3: At the assailant's grasp, keep your balance. Step wide and circularly to your right rear with your right foot, bringing your back and right shoulder into hard contact with the assailant's right elbow. (See

lower diagram, page 82, and lower left picture.) Draw your right foot in toward your left leg, weighting your left leg and lifting your right leg high by bending it at the knee. Watch your assailant carefully. (See picture, lower right.) Drive your right leg in a stamping action to his knee, shin, or instep, using your Foot Edge hard against the target. This action can be seen on page 84.

Key Points: During your striking action in Response 1, it is not necessary to shift your weight onto your left leg (toward the assailant), but it is necessary that your head be turned toward the assailant in order to properly gauge the strike. In the formation of your Knife-hand, be sure to keep your fingers together with the thumb tucked tightly to your forefinger.

In Response 2, center your weight on the right leg as you drive your foot edge into the target. Too much lean away from the assailant will lessen the effect against shin and arch. If you lean, it is better to select the assailant's knee as your target.

In Response 3, the stamping leg thigh must be raised parallel to the ground. Notice that your hips must be twisted to the right rear to permit proper kicking action.

Situation: While you are seated you are attacked by an assailant who has grasped your collar from the side and rear. He is attempting to strike you.

Response: At the assailant's grasp from the side and rear, turn to meet his glance, keeping your right arm ready for action. Keep your seat and your balance. (See picture, page 85.)

As the assailant tugs to pull you up and out of your chair, or as he begins to strike you with his free hand, raise your right arm, hand held in a tight fist, knuckles upward, so that it is parallel to the ground, elbow pointing at your assailant's mid-section. (See picture above.)

If your assailant's striking action is imminent, swing your arm upward in a whipping action, pivoting on your elbow, keeping the knuckles of your tight fist facing your assailant. (See picture, page 87.)

Slam your Back Fist hard into the assailant's face area by a whipping action of your striking arm. Withdraw your left arm alongside your body, hand in a tight fist, knuckles down at your left hip. Keep this ready for a counterattack. This striking action can be seen on page 88.

Key Points: Timing your attack is essential and must be done a split second before the assailant strikes you. If you are pulled out of your chair by the assailant, time this with the force of your striking.

An alternate target area is the assailant's groin or solar plexus.

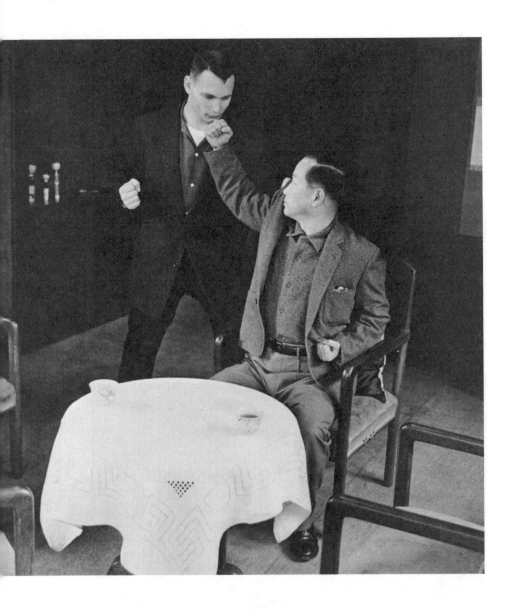

Situation: An assailant has taken your left arm into a hammer lock with his left hand and is holding your collar with his right hand. He is about to force you forward. You have plenty of room to move about.

89

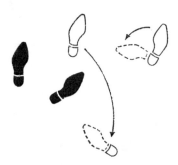

Response: As he forces you forward, keep your balance as much as possible. (See page 89.) Shift your weight to your right leg and as your weight comes on to that foot, pivot it slightly to your left as you step your left foot back diagonally to the side of the assailant's right foot. See diagram.

This action will twist your body to the left and prepare you for a striking attack against the assailant. Your hips are lowered, legs braced, and weight centered. (See picture to the left.)

As you step back with your left foot and twist your body, do not tug to release your trapped left arm, but make use of the circular body action to bring your left hand out from behind your body, fingers pointing upward, pivoting it on the elbow as your twist your body. Do not tug to release yourself, but use the elbow as a pivot as you snap your left arm upward, palm toward the assailant. (See lower picture this page and left picture on page 91.) Notice that your feet stay in place during this motion.

As your left hand comes up free, grasp the assailant's left arm and pull him off balance to your left rear corner, using the twist of your body to assist this. (See right picture above.)

Strike your assailant in the solar plexus area with your right elbow by twisting your body more and driving your elbow hard into the target area. This action can be seen on page 92.

Key Points: The striking action must be coordinated with the stepping and twisting of your body to the left. Shift your weight to your now advanced left foot as your strike.

92

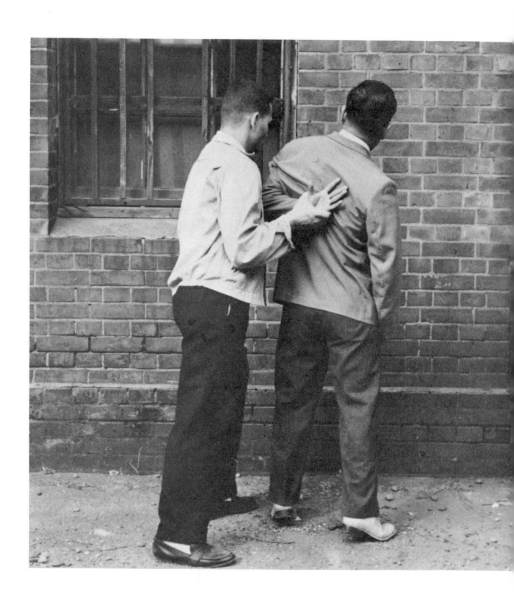

Situation: An assailant has taken you into a hammer lock using your left arm, and is forcing you up against a wall. You have very little room to move forward.

93

Response: Pull your trapped arm tightly against your back. (See left picture.) Wait until his hammer lock pressure is somewhat relaxed and then quickly step backward slightly to your right side with your right foot as in the diagram.

Twist your body to the right as far as you can and bring your right arm into the position shown below. During this action you must keep your balance and watch your assailant carefully.

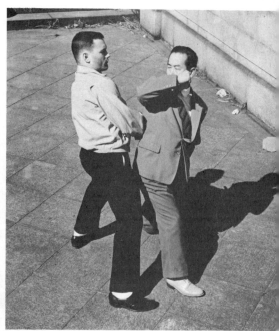

In the picture above, note that your right arm which is coming into position for a counterattack is raised with the elbow high.

Strike the assailant in the face area with your right Back or Bottom Fist by passing your right arm forcibly over his right arm which is applying the hammer lock. This action can be seen on page 96.

95

Key Points: Before you begin your twist and stepping action, pull your trapped arm tightly to your back and try to time your movement with the moment his hammer lock is somewhat relaxed.

96

Situation: An assailant has taken a judo wrist lock from your rear and is attempting to force you to the ground. You have plenty of room to move about.

97

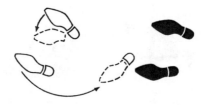

Response: As your assailant takes your wrist, keep your balance and put moderate resistance into your captured arm. (See picture, page 97.) Quickly pivot your right foot slightly to your left and step your left foot backward to a new position just inside of your assailant's left foot, your toes pointing at his toes. See diagram. Raise your left arm, begin to form a fist, knuckles outward or upward. (See picture on page 99.)

Twist your body to your rearmost leg, swinging your Bottom Fist in an arc hard against your assailant's ribs or kidney area, using your tight Bottom Fist as a striking point. This action can be seen on page 100.

Key Points: Your stepping, body shifting, and striking action must be timed with the twist of your body to make this response effective. If you begin this action too late, this response may not work at all.

100

Situation: You are jumped from behind and the assailant has taken you into a Full Nelson hold. You have plenty of room to move about.

Response 1: As your assailant takes his Full Nelson hold, keep your balance as best you can. (See top right picture.) If he tries to break you backward, lean hard forward and begin to swing both your arms downward, fists tightly clenched together. (Follow picture sequence to the left.) Butt him backward with your buttocks.

Bring the large knuckles of your middle fingers of your fists directly into his rib area. Quickly twist and swing the assailant around your body to either side (right shown). Repeated striking in his ribs with your knuckles and violent twisting of your body may loosen his attack.

Response 2: As your assailant takes his Full Nelson hold, keep your balance as in the top picture.

Shift your weight to your left leg and raise your right leg so that your thigh is parallel to the ground, as shown in the picture below.

Drive your raised foot downward hard against your assailant's shin or instep, using the Foot Edge of your right shoe as your striking point. This action can be seen on page 104.

Key Points: Response 1 is a moderate form of punishment which should discourage an ordinary assailant from further action; however, in extreme cases, response 2 is justified.

It is possible that your counterattack may loosen his Full Nelson and cause him to merely hug his arms around your body in an attempt to pick you up or squeeze you into submission. In this case, drive the knuckle of your middle finger, extended from your fist, into the back of his hand. If his grasp is loose, swing your body around and bring your elbow hard into his face or head area. Both of these actions are shown on page 104.

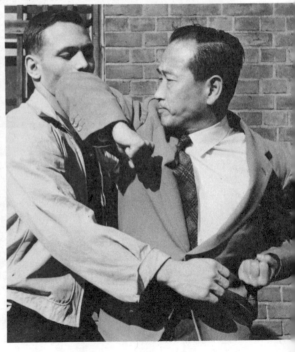

Situation: An assailant attacks you by surprise from the rear in a "mugging" fashion, encircling your neck with his left arm in an attempt to choke you. You have plenty of room to move about.

Response: At the assailant's attack, keep your balance as best you can. (See upper picture.) Immediately step diagonally forward and outward with your left foot, toes pointing slightly to the right, and shift your weight to that foot, as shown in the diagram.

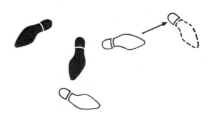

As your weight centers on your advanced left foot, twist your hips to the right as you fold your right arm across your body and make a Knife-hand as shown in the picture to the left.

Swing your Knife-hand downward in an arc which pivots on the elbow. This action is toward your rear and is shown above.

Strike your assailant with your Knife-hand as a striking point, hard to his groin area by twisting your body with the force of the Knife-hand blow. This action may be seen on page 108.

Key Points: This stepping, shifting of body weight, twisting of your body, and the striking action must be blended into one smooth movement for maximum effect. Turn your head with the striking action of your arm in order to properly gauge the target. An alternate striking point is the Bottom Fist.

108

Situation: An assailant has attacked you from the rear with a bear hug. You have plenty of room to move about.

109

Response 1: As your assailant grasps you from the rear, keep your balance and try to butt him with the back of your head. (See upper picture.)

Quickly step circularly forward with your left foot as shown in the diagram, driving your arms forward and outward as your weight shifts forward. (See picture below.) Lower your hips with the shift of your weight and clench your fists.

Twist your body to your right (toward the rearmost foot) turning your head so as to look at the assailant's mid section. Raise your left arm high and begin to drive your right elbow toward your assailant's mid section. Your left arm drives a hard Forefist into the facial or head area of the assailant. This action can be seen on page 112.

Response 2: As your assailant grasps you from the rear, somewhat higher than in response 1, keep your balance and try to butt him with the back of your head.

Quickly lunge forward with your left foot, throwing both of your arms forward and upward. (See pictures, lower left.)

Bring your right elbow hard into your assailant's mid section and your left Fore Fist into his facial or head area by twisting as you did in response 1. This action can be seen on page 112.

Key Points: Your stepping, weight shift, and hip twist must be in time with your striking action if this response is to be effective. Be sure to turn your striking arm so that on contact with your target, the knuckles of your left fist are pointing upward.

Your left arm and the striking Fore Fist need not be employed, but may be left in the position shown in the picture below.

An alternate punishment is to drive your heel or foot edge into the assailant's arch or shin. See the picture at the beginning of this chapter (page 79).

If your assailant makes his attack without containing your arms, you can loosen his grasp and stop his attack by driving the knuckle of your middle finger, extended from your fist, into the back of his hand, as shown on page 104. As his grasp loosens, swing your body to the right and bring your elbow hard into his face or head.

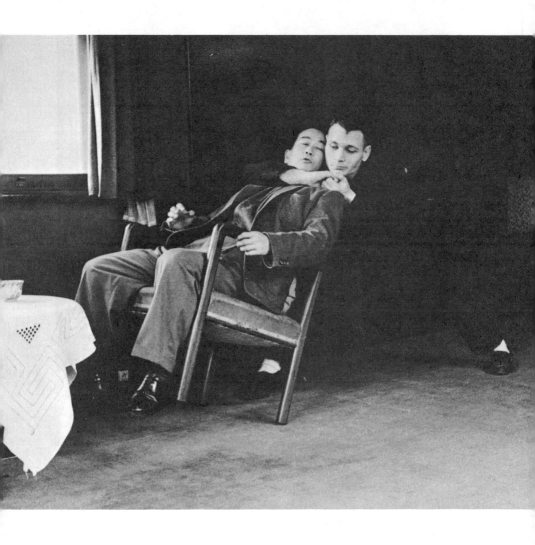

Situation: An assailant is attempting to choke you from behind as you sit on a chair.

113

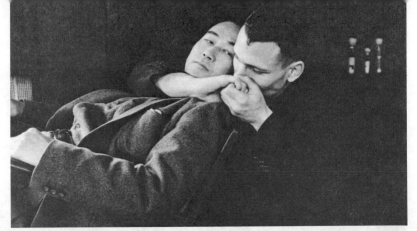

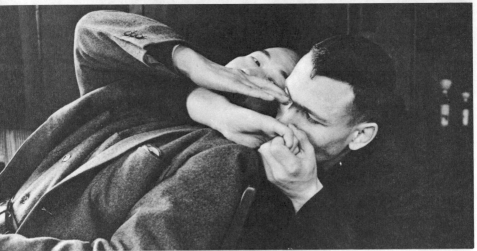

Response 1: Keep your seat. Do not try to get up or break loose from the assailant's grasp by standing up. This is especially true if he has broken your balance by tilting your chair backward, as shown on page 113.

Make an effort to turn your face away from his elbow. If his face is sufficiently exposed, drive a Hand Spear formed by the hand and fingers of your hand opposite to the side on which the assailant's head is located (right hand shown above). Drive repeated attacks into his face area, aiming for his eyes.

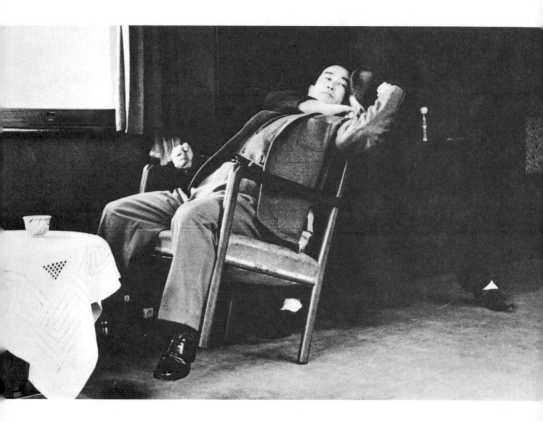

Response 2: Keep your seat. Do not try to get up or break loose from the assailant's grasp by standing up. This is especially true if he has broken your balance by tilting your chair backward.

Make an effort to turn your face away from his elbow. If his face is somewhat protected and difficult to attack with your Hand Spear, use the extended knuckle of your middle finger, hand formed as a fist (see picture above) to strike the face and head area of your assailant. Drive repeated attacks to his face and head area, aiming for his temple. For formation of the fist, see the diagram.

Key Points: Struggling to stand up after being seized from behind as you sit on a chair is generally pointless. Rather allow yourself to be kept in the chair and counterattack immediately as suggested.

Turning toward the assailant's head shortens and improves the distance to the target, thus facilitating your attack.

Additional effect may be gotten by catching hold of the assailant's head with your left arm, immobilizing it, and making it a better target for your attack with your Hand Spear in response 1.

Situation: An assailant is attempting to strike you with a straight right hand punch to your head from the side as you sit on a chair.

117

Response: Keep your seat. Do not try to get up to avoid the punch. Keep your assailant in view and both your hands ready, as shown on page 117.

As the assailant throws his punch, twist quickly in your chair, bracing your feet on the floor, facing your assailant and raising both your hands to intercept his punch. Your left hand, palm open and facing to your right, is placed ahead of and crossed over your right hand with the palm facing to your left. See pictures above. Use your left hand to grasp and deflect the assailant's punching right arm away from your head or face area by directing it outward and to your left rear by a sharp, strong pull. Simultaneously, as your right hand is freed, make a tight fist as shown on page 119.

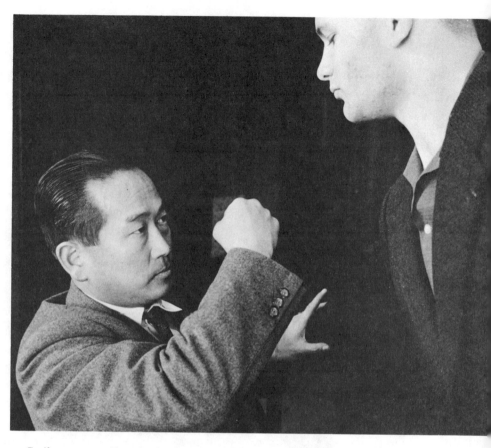

Strike your assailant in the face area (chin, mouth, nose) by delivering a hard Back or Bottom Fist blow. During this action, keep your feet in place. This striking can be seen on page 120.

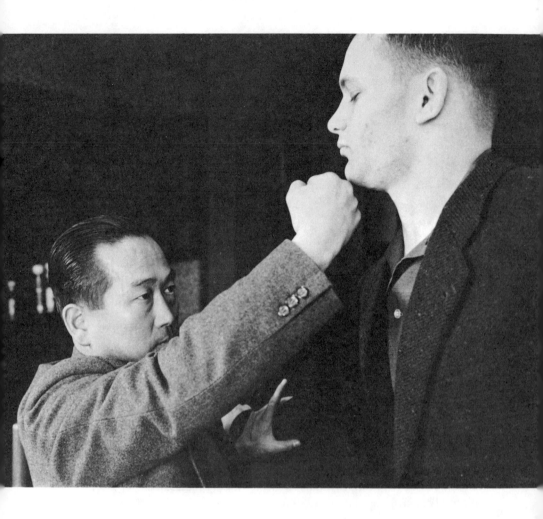

Key Points: The feet must be braced strongly on the ground as you twist to face the assailant and deliver your striking action. Notice in the pictures on page 118 that your right hand may be used to ward off a blow from the left hand of the assailant if necessary, prior to striking.